C000139187

This book belongs to

Age

Favourite player

Prediction of Blues' final position this season

Prediction of Sky Bet Championship winners this season

Prediction of FA Cup winners this season

Prediction of Capital One Cup winners this season

Prediction of teams to be promoted
to the Barclays Premier League this season

1st

2nd

Play-off Winners

Written by twocan

A TWOCAN PUBLICATION

©2013. Published by twocan
under licence from Birmingham City FC.

ISBN 978-1-909872-00-4

PICTURE CREDITS
Press Association

£6.99

CONTENTS

PROPERTY OF B

ELECTRONIC CIGARETTES

BACK ROW: Joe Carnall, Jon Seeley, Hayden Mullins, Neal Eardley, Kyle Bartley, Dan Burn, Nikola Zigic, Will Packwood, Tom Adeyemi, Callum Reilly, Jonathan Spector, Pete Shaw, Steve Watson

MIDDLE ROW: Tom Page, Denis Butler, Ryan Higgins, Reece Hales, David Murphy, Lee Novak, Colin Doyle, Nick Townsend, Darren Randolph, Matt Green, Darren Ambrose, Andy Shinnie, Amari'i Bell, James Fry, Paul Doherty, Dr. Mike Stone

FRONT ROW: John Vaughan, Dave Hunt, Peter Lovenkrands, Charlee Adams, Scott Allan, Mitch Hancox, Olly Lee, Paul Robinson, Derek Fazackerly, Lee Clark, Terry McDermott, Wade Elliott, Chris Burke, Shane Ferguson, Koby Arthur, Liam Truslove, Richard Beale, Dr. Tom Little, Chris Hancock

FITNESS

Footballers are top athletes. In order to stay at the top of their game they need to be supremely fit. Unlike sports such as athletics, cricket, tennis or basketball for instance football is a contact sport which means that as well as injuries that can be picked up through strains or pulls, footballers have to deal with the rough and tumble of applying their skills when they often only have a split second between gaining possession of the ball and having to withstand a challenge, often one that can injure them.

Once footballers hear the final whistle attention swiftly turns to the next game which in the Sky Bet Championship usually comes every few days. The result of this is that not only do players have to be fantastically fit but they have to perform time and time again with at least 48 games to be played each season, more if teams do not lose at the first hurdle in the cup competitions.

Footballers do a lot of running, weight training and swimming. They might also go cycling and more and more clubs now get players to 'box-er-cise' which involves a lot of routines normally done by boxers. Pilates and yoga can also be beneficial for players because such activities help to stretch muscles, assist with back problems and increase body strength.

Most of the hard work done by players is carried out in the pre-season period. This is when fitness and conditioning coaches work on building-up players so that they can perform for 90 minutes against a team of opponents all of whom they can expect to be super-fit too.

Once the season gets going, most clubs train for around two hours a day with much of the training based on actually playing, particularly focussing on the next match they have to play. It is important that during the season players don't over-train. Rest and recuperation can be as important as a weights session because fitness coaches have to ensure player performance peaks for matchday.

FIRST

THE ONE & ONLY
GIL MERRICK

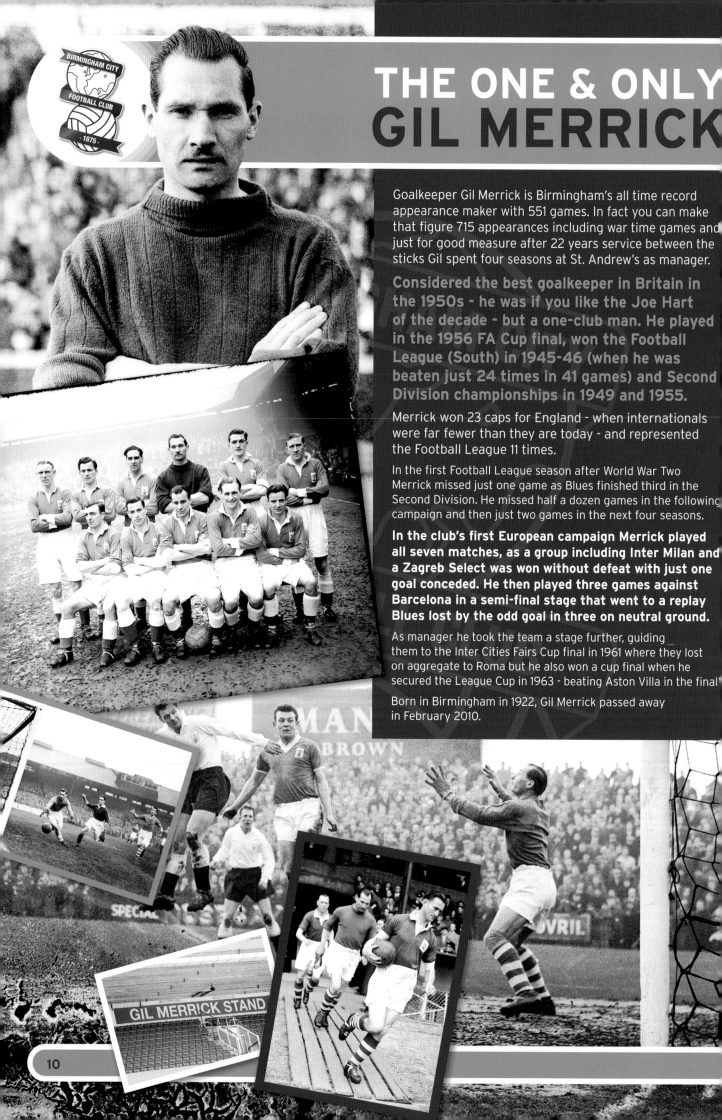

Goalkeeper Gil Merrick is Birmingham's all time record appearance maker with 551 games. In fact you can make that figure 715 appearances including war time games and just for good measure after 22 years service between the sticks Gil spent four seasons at St. Andrew's as manager.

Considered the best goalkeeper in Britain in the 1950s - he was if you like the Joe Hart of the decade - but a one-club man. He played in the 1956 FA Cup final, won the Football League (South) in 1945-46 (when he was beaten just 24 times in 41 games) and Second Division championships in 1949 and 1955.

Merrick won 23 caps for England - when internationals were far fewer than they are today - and represented the Football League 11 times.

In the first Football League season after World War Two Merrick missed just one game as Blues finished third in the Second Division. He missed half a dozen games in the following campaign and then just two games in the next four seasons.

In the club's first European campaign Merrick played all seven matches, as a group including Inter Milan and a Zagreb Select was won without defeat with just one goal conceded. He then played three games against Barcelona in a semi-final stage that went to a replay Blues lost by the odd goal in three on neutral ground.

As manager he took the team a stage further, guiding them to the Inter Cities Fairs Cup final in 1961 where they lost on aggregate to Roma but he also won a cup final when he secured the League Cup in 1963 - beating Aston Villa in the final.

Born in Birmingham in 1922, Gil Merrick passed away in February 2010.

GIL MERRICK STAND

6 DAN BURN

3

1

Darren Randolph

Position: Goalkeeper
Nationality: Irish
DOB: 12th May 1987
Height: 6'1" (185.4cm)
Weight: 12st 3lbs (77.5kg)

The Republic of Ireland international joined Blues on 1 July 2013, after leaving Motherwell, following three seasons with the SPL club.

David Murphy

Position: Defender
Nationality: English
DOB: 1st March 1984
Height: 6'0" (183cm)
Weight: 13st 3lbs (84kg)

Murphy started the 2012/13 campaign in good form but suffered a knee injury in November 2012, which sidelined him for the remainder of the season. He hopes to be back on top form this season.

2

Neal Eardley

Position: Defender
Nationality: Welsh
DOB: 6th November 1988
Height: 5'11" (180cm)
Weight: 11st 8lbs (73.54kg)

The Wales international moved to Blues in the summer of 2013 after his contract with Blackpool came to an end. He made his Blues debut at home to Watford on 3 August but suffered a serious knee injury at the end of that same month.

THE SQUAD 2013·14

4

Paul Robinson

Position: Defender
Nationality: English
DOB: 17th December 1978
Height: 5'9" (175cm)
Weight: 12st 9lbs (80.3kg)

Robinson made 37 appearances last season and ahead of the 2013/14 campaign was given the role of both club and team captain by boss Lee Clark!

5

Kyle Bartley

Position: Defender
Nationality: English
DOB: 22nd May 1991
Height: 6'4" (194cm)
Weight: 14st 11lbs (94kg)

Blues swooped to sign Swansea City's highly-rated defender Bartley in July 2013 on a season-long loan deal.

Chris Burke

Position: Midfielder
Nationality: Scottish
DOB: 2nd December 1983
Height: 5'9" (175cm)
Weight: 10st 10lbs (68kg)

After six years without international recognition, Burke was named in Gordon Strachan's first squad in January 2013! According to Strachan, "Chris was fantastic in the Europa League at a good level, he has a maturity about his play now..."

6

Dan Burn

Position: Defender
Nationality: English
DOB: 9th May 1992
Height: 6'6" (198cm)
Weight: 13st 10lbs (87kg)

Promising Fulham centre-back Dan Burn joined Blues in July 2013 on a season-long loan.

7

8 10

Darren Ambrose

Position: Midfielder
Nationality: English
DOB: 29th February 1984
Height: 6'0" (183cm)
Weight: 12st 2lbs (77.1kg)

Ambrose signed a two-year deal in July 2012 but a knee injury kept him out most of last term, he's looking good for the rest of this season!

Hayden Mullins

Position: Midfielder
Nationality: English
DOB: 27th March 1979
Height: 5'11" (180.3cm)
Weight: 10st 7lbs (66.6kg)
Experienced midfielder Hayden Mullins joined Blues from Portsmouth in July 2012, he can also play as a defensive sweeper or right-back.

11

Peter Lovenkrands

Position: Striker
Nationality: Danish
DOB: 29th January 1980
Height: 5'10" (179cm)
Weight: 12st 3lbs (77.4kg)
Lovenkrands is a striker who can also play as a left winger and is known for his pace. He has made over 20 appearances for Denmark and he won the 1998 Danish Under-19 Player of the Year award.

12

13

Lee Novak

Position: Striker
Nationality: English
DOB: 28th September 1988
Height: 6'0" (183cm)
Weight: 12st 4lbs (78kg)

A tall and powerful striker, Novak joined Blues in the summer of 2013 on a three-year deal after his contract at Huddersfield Town expired. Blues boss Lee Clark was well aware of Novak's capabilities having plucked the free-scoring Geordie out of non-league to sign for Huddersfield back in January 2009!

Colin Doyle

Position: Goalkeeper
Nationality: Irish
DOB: 12th June 1985
Height: 6'5" (195.5cm)
Weight: 14st 5lbs (91.1kg)

Colin Doyle came over from Ireland to join the club as a 16-year-old Academy scholar in 2001. He signed a new two-year deal in the summer of 2013.

14

Wade Elliott

Position: Midfielder
Nationality: English
DOB: 14th December 1978
Height: 5'10" (178cm)
Weight: 10st 3lbs (64.9kg)

A talented and reliable midfielder, Elliott is a mainstay in the first team and made 38 league appearances last season.

Will Packwood

Position: Defender
Nationality: American
DOB: 21st May 1993
Height: 6'3" (191cm)
Weight: 12st 8lbs (80kg)

Packwood has represented the United States at U20 level and he signed a one-year contract extension with Blues in the summer of 2013.

15

16

Koby Arthur

Position: Midfielder
Nationality: Ghanaian
DOB: 3rd January 1996
Height: 5'6" (168cm)
Weight: 10st 10lbs (68kg)

The highly-rated Ghanaian youngster has been with Blues since 2012. He is a powerful striker of the ball and can play any across the middle of the park or in a more advanced role.

17

Callum Reilly

Position: Midfielder
Nationality: English
DOB: 3rd October 1993
Height: 6'1" (185cm)
Weight: 12st 4lbs (78kg)

Reilly is a product of Blues' Academy. He made his first team debut as a second-half substitute during Blues' FA Cup fourth round victory against Sheffield United in January 2012.

18

Mitch Hancox

Position: Defender
Nationality: English
DOB: 9th November 1993
Height: 5'10" (177.8cm)
Weight: 11st 3lbs (71.2kg)

Solihull-born Hancox has been with Blues since joining the Academy at just eight. He predominantly plays at left-back, but can also play on the left of midfield.

19

Nikola Zigic

Position: Striker
Nationality: Serbian
DOB: 25th Sept 1980
Height: 6'8" (203cm)
Weight: 15st 2lbs (96kg)

The towering Serbian international scored nine times in 36 appearances last season.

21

20

Olly Lee

Position: Midfielder
Nationality: English
DOB: 11th July 1991
Height: 5'11" (181cm)
Weight: 12st 8lbs (80kg)

Lee signed a one-year contract with Blues in the summer of 2013, with a further one-year option. He is the son of former Newcastle and England midfielder Rob Lee.

Akwasi Asante

Position: Striker
Nationality: Dutch
DOB: 6th Sept 1992
Height: 6'0" (183cm)
Weight: 13st 1lbs (83kg)

A promising striker, Asante was signed to the Blues' Academy at the age of 13. He penned a new one-year deal with Blues in the summer of 2013.

22

Andy Shinnie

Position: Midfielder
Nationality: Scottish
DOB: 17th July 1989
Height: 5'11" (180.3cm)
Weight: 11st 0lbs (70kg)

Former Inverness Caledonian Thistle midfielder Shinnie joined Blues in the summer of 2013. His performances for ICT saw him nominated for the PFA Scotland Player of the Year award.

Jonathan Spector

Position: Midfielder
Nationality: American
DOB: 1st March 1986
Height: 6'0" (182cm)
Weight: 12st 6lbs (79kg)

Spector signed a new two-year deal with Blues in the summer of 2013. He has also made over 30 appearances for the United States.

23

24

Tom Adeyemi

Position: Midfielder
Nationality: English
DOB: 24th October 1991
Height: 6'1" (186cm)
Weight: 13st 5lbs (85kg)

Blues signed exciting young midfielder Tom Adeyemi on a two-year deal in the summer of 2013.

25

Matt Green

Position: Striker
Nationality: English
DOB: 2nd January 1987
Height: 6'0" (183cm)
Weight: 12st 11lbs (81kg)

Green joined Blues in July 2013 on a two-year contract. Lee Clark moved quickly to sign the hottest property in non-league football following his impressive scoring record for Mansfield Town.

26

Scott Allan

Position: Midfielder
Nationality: Scottish
DOB: 28th November 1991
Height: 5'9" (175cm)
Weight: 12st 4lbs (77.9kg)

The Scotland U21 international joined Blues in July 2013 on a season-long loan. He made his debut as a second-half substitute at home to Watford on 3 August, and scored twice as Birmingham beat Plymouth Argyle 3-2 after extra time in the League Cup three days later.

Shane Ferguson

Position: Midfielder
Nationality: Northern Irish
DOB: 12th February 1991
Height: 5'6" (168cm)
Weight: 10st 4lbs (65.1kg)

Blues signed Ferguson on a season-long loan in July 2013. The left-sider is equally as comfortable playing on the wing or at full-back.

27

Ryan Higgins

29

Position: Midfielder
Nationality: English
DOB: 1st May 1994
Height: 5'9" (175cm)
Weight: 12st 0lbs (76kg)

Higgins' solid performances during the 2012/13 campaign with the Blues development squad saw him rewarded with a 12-month professional contract, plus a 12-month option in the summer of 2013!

Reece Brown

Position: Midfielder
Nationality: English
DOB: 3rd March 1996
Height: 5'9" (175cm)
Weight: 12st 4lbs (77.9kg)

Brown has been with the club since the age of ten and progressed through the Academy ranks. He made his non-competitive debut for the first-team at the age of just 17, when he came on as a substitute during the 2-1 pre-season victory over Hull City in August 2013.

28

30

Nick Townsend

Position: Goalkeeper
Nationality: English
DOB: 1st November 1994
Height: 5'11" (181cm)
Weight: 14st 5lbs (91kg)

A product of Blues' Academy, goalkeeper Nick Townsend signed for Blues at the age of 12 and signed a pro-contract last summer!

31

Paul Caddis

Position: Defender
Nationality: Scottish
DOB: 19th April 1988
Height: 5'7" (170cm)
Weight: 10st 8lbs (67kg)

Caddis signed a three year contract with Blues on 2 September 2013 after performing well on loan at Blues last season.

Set up three cones in a large triangle. These become our three goals! Make sure the triangle is big enough for the goalie to dive around in.

The goalie stands in the centre of the triangle and three shooters stand opposite the three goals at their 'penalty spots'.

EASY

To start with, the shooters take it in turns to fire shots past the goalie - the goalie must work quickly to reposition himself for the next shot.

HARD

Players then start to fire shots more quickly. Just as the goalkeeper recovers from the last shot, the next player quickly shoots again.

HARDER

Change the order in which the shooters take their shots.

This drill is very tiring for the keeper. Remember to swap positions so that everyone gets the chance to be in goal.

Shooters shout their names in any order, to signal that they are going to shoot. This keeps the goalie on his toes.

Also, be sure to try different shots - high, low, left foot, right foot, maybe even try chipping the ball over the keeper's head!

DRILLS: GOALKEEPING

Each creature represents a football club...
can you name every one?

1

2

3

4

5

6

7

8

WILD
ABOUT
FOOTIE

9

10

ANSWERS ON PAGE 62

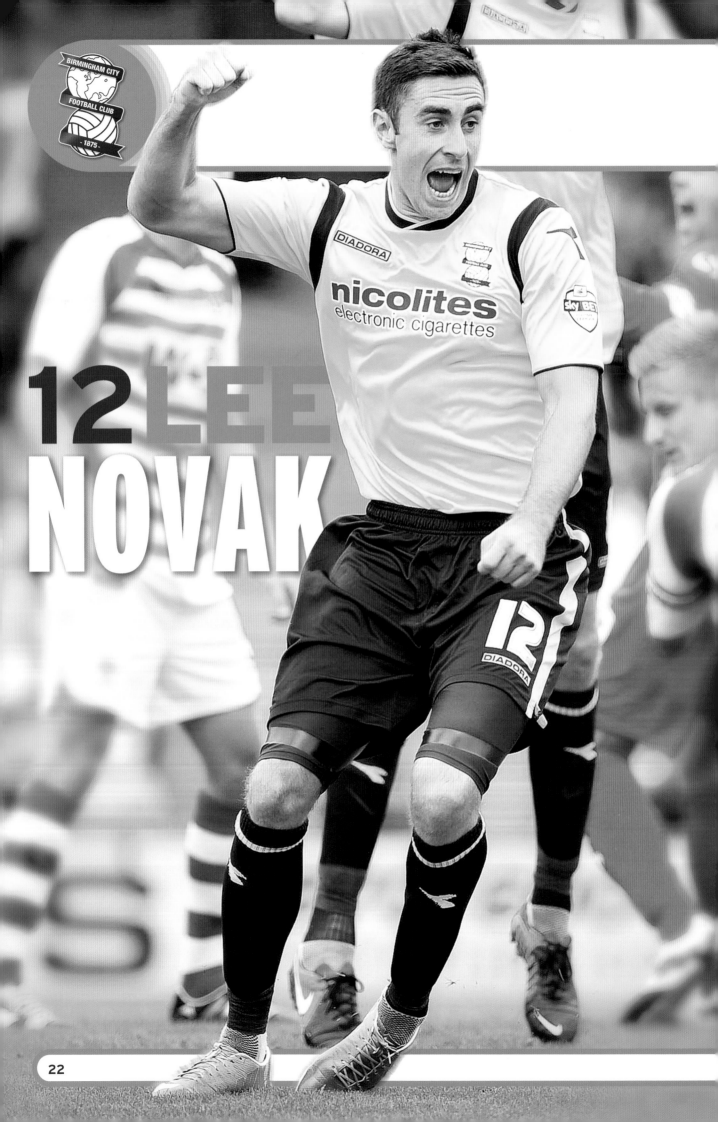

12 LEE NOVAK

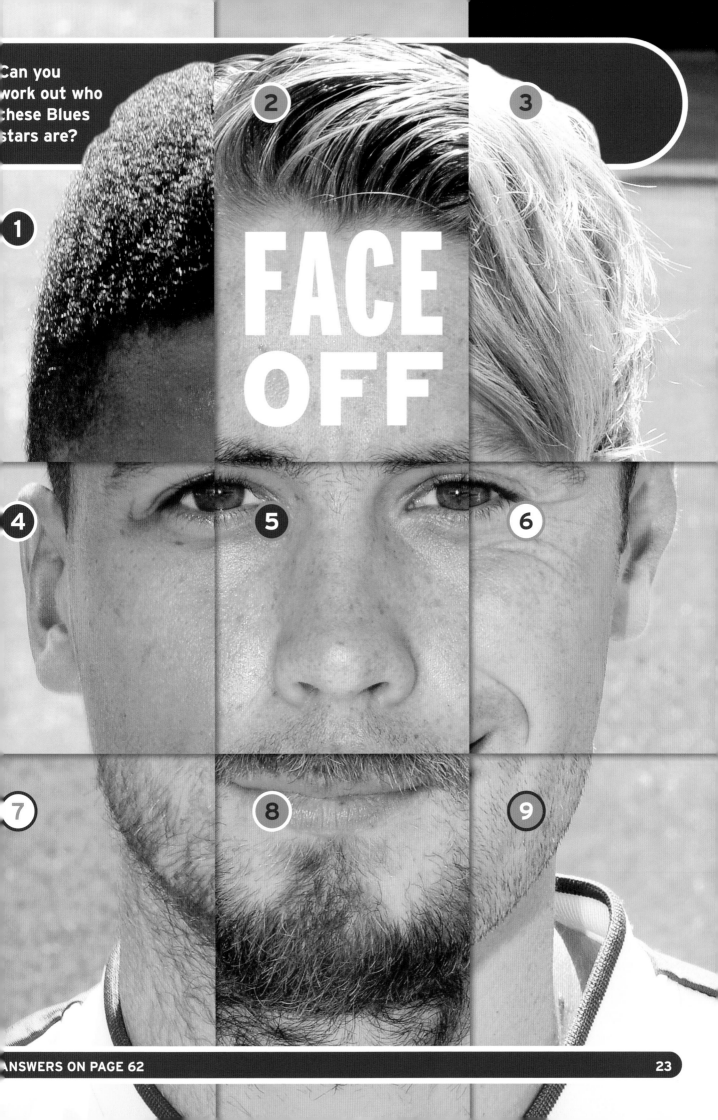

FACE OFF

1
2
3
4
5
6
7
8
9

MEET YOUR RIVALS

BARNSLEY

GROUND: Oakwell CAPACITY: 23,009
MANAGER: David Flitcroft NICKNAMES: The Tykes, The Reds
DID YOU KNOW: Barnsley have spent more seasons in the second tier of English football than any other club in history!

BLACKBURN ROVERS

GROUND: Ewood Park CAPACITY: 31,367 MANAGER: Gary Bowyer
NICKNAMES: Rovers, Blue and Whites, The Riversiders
DID YOU KNOW: Blackburn Rovers' Latin motto is 'Arte et labore', the club's translation of which is 'By Skill and Hard Work'.

BLACKPOOL

GROUND: Bloomfield Road CAPACITY: 17,338
MANAGER: Paul Ince NICKNAMES: The Seasiders, The 'Pool, The Tangerines DID YOU KNOW: Blackpool's most notable achievement is winning the 1953 FA Cup Final.

BOLTON WANDERERS

GROUND: Reebok Stadium CAPACITY: 28,723
MANAGER: Dougie Freedman NICKNAMES: The Trotters,The Whites, The White Men, The Men in White DID YOU KNOW: Bolton have won the FA Cup four times - 1923, 1926, 1929 and 1958.

AFC BOURNEMOUTH

GROUND: Dean Court CAPACITY: 10,783 MANAGER: Eddie Howe
NICKNAMES: The Cherries, Boscombe DID YOU KNOW: Last season, Bournemouth won promotion to the Championship putting them in the second tier of the league for only the second time in their history.

BRIGHTON & HOVE ALBION

GROUND: The Amex CAPACITY: 30,750 HEAD COACH: Óscar García
NICKNAMES: The Seagulls, The Albion DID YOU KNOW: Brighton has a number of celebrity fans, including commentator, Des Lynam, DJ, Fat Boy Slim and comic genius, Norman Wisdom.

PART1

Time to get to grips with the teams Birmingham City will be facing this season...

BURNLEY

GROUND: Turf Moor **CAPACITY:** 22,546 **MANAGER:** Sean Dyche
NICKNAME: The Clarets **DID YOU KNOW:** Burnley are one of only two teams to have won all top four professional divisions of English football - the other team being Wolverhampton Wanderers.

CHARLTON ATHLETIC

GROUND: The Valley **CAPACITY:** 27,111 **MANAGER:** Chris Powell
NICKNAME: The Addicks **DID YOU KNOW:** Charlton were rare among football clubs, they used to reserve a seat on their directors' board for a supporter! (until 2008, when legal issues stopped them)

DERBY COUNTY

GROUND: Pride Park Stadium **CAPACITY:** 33 597
MANAGER: Nigel Clough **NICKNAME:** The Rams
DID YOU KNOW: Derby County are one of only ten clubs to have competed in every season of the English football league!

DONCASTER ROVERS

GROUND: Keepmoat Stadium **CAPACITY:** 15,231
MANAGER: Paul Dickov **NICKNAMES:** The Rovers, Donny
DID YOU KNOW: Doncaster won promotion from League One last season with a number one finish!

HUDDERSFIELD TOWN

GROUND: John Smith's Stadium **CAPACITY:** 24,500 **MANAGER:** Mark Robins
NICKNAME: The Terriers **DID YOU KNOW:** In 1926, Huddersfield became the first English team to win three successive league titles - no team has beaten this record and only three teams have matched it (Arsenal, Liverpool and Man United).

BIG FAT QUIZ OF THE

**Who scored Blues'
first goal of the
2012-13 season?**

1.

**Who was Blues'
top scorer of the
2012-13 season?**

2.

**Who was
Blues' top league
appearance
maker of the
2012-13 season?**

3.

**Who scored the
first goal of 2013?**

4.

**What was the
highest home
attendance last
season and who
did we play?**

5.

Which team did Blues beat in the League Cup last season?

6.

How many league games ended in a draw last season?

7.

Which Blues player only has their birthday on a leap year and will celebrate their 30th this coming year?

8.

Which two players received the most yellow cards last season?

9.

What position did Blues finish last season?

10.

BACK CHAT

MATT GREEN

YOUR TEAM MATES

Who is the best trainer? Paul Robinson
Who has the worst dress sense? Probably me
Who is the best dancer? Koby Arthur
Who is the joker in the dressing room? Andy Shinnie
Who spends longest in front of the mirror?
Chris Burke or Jonathan Spector

FAVOURITES

Favourite actor?
Denzel Washington
Favourite actress?
Angelina Jolie
Favourite movie?
Man on Fire
Favourite musician or band?
Bob Marley
Favourite place? Jamaica

What do you do on your days off? **Sleep**

If you could trade places with someone for a day, who would it be? **Barack Obama**

What are your pet hates? **Liars**

Snow or (Sun?)
(Coffee)or tea?
(Early bird) or night owl?
(Action) or comedy?
Apple or (Blackberry?)
(Cowboys) or aliens?
Sausage or (bacon?)
Cats or (dogs?)
Bond or (Bourne?)

If not a footballer, what would you be? **Basketball player**

What do you do on your days off? **Sleep & eat**

What are your pet hates? **Traffic**

Snow or (Sun?)
(Coffee) or tea?
Early bird or (night owl?)
(Action) or comedy?
(Apple) or Blackberry?
(Cowboys) or aliens?
Sausage or (bacon?)
Cats or (dogs?)
(Bond) or Bourne?

DARREN RANDOLPH

YOUR TEAM MATES

Who is the best trainer? Paul Robinson
Who has the worst dress sense? Ha ha, I'll be losing friends here. Not necessarily the worst but a few outfits that I've thought are brave have been worn by Wade Elliott.
Who is the best dancer? From the moves that I saw during pre-season, I'll say Mitch Hancox, Olly Lee and Andy Shinnie.
Who is the joker in the dressing room? Paul Robinson, Wade Elliott or Nikola Zigic
Who spends longest in front of the mirror? Wade Elliott

FAVOURITES

Favourite actor? Denzel Washington
Favourite actress?
There's a few - Megan Fox, Jessica Alba
Favourite movie? Scarface
Favourite musician or band?
Michael Jackson
Favourite place? Miami

JONATHAN SPECTOR

YOUR TEAM MATES

Who is the best trainer? Lee Novak

Who has the worst dress sense? I'm not going there, you just can't win!

Who is the best dancer? I haven't seen the lads dance so I can't say but I know it's not me.

Who is the joker in the dressing room? Paul Robinson

Who spends longest in front of the mirror? Wade Elliott for sure!

FAVOURITES

Favourite actor? Johnny Depp

Favourite actress? Kiera Knightley

Favourite movie? Snatch

Favourite musician or band? Rolling Stones

Favourite place? Chicago

What do you do on your days off?
My wife and I like to see the country. We've been to the Cotswolds, London and Manchester and hope to see Bath at some point if the schedule permits.

If not a footballer, what would you be?
Architect

Snow or Sun?
Coffee or tea?
Early bird or night owl?
Action or comedy?
Apple or Blackberry?
Cowboys or aliens?
Sausage or bacon?
Cats or dogs?
Bond or Bourne?

If you were a character in any movie, who would it be?
Johnny Depp in Pirates of the Caribbean.

CHRIS BURKE

YOUR TEAM MATES

Who is the best trainer? Paul Robinson

Who has the worst dress sense? Colin Doyle

Who is the best dancer? Wade Elliott

Who is the joker in the dressing room? Paul Robinson

Who spends longest in front of the mirror? Wade Elliott

FAVOURITES

Favourite actor? Will Ferrell

Favourite actress? Jennifer Lawrence

Favourite movie? Scarface

Favourite musician or band? Jay-Z

Favourite place? My house

What are your pet hates?
Stairs

If not a footballer, what would you be?
Property developer

What do you do on your days off?
Drink coffee

Snow or Sun?
Coffee or tea?
Early bird or night owl?
Action or comedy?
Apple or Blackberry?
Cowboys or aliens?
Sausage or bacon?
Cats or dogs? neither
Bond or Bourne?

CAN YOU MANAGE?

The surnames of former Blues managers, dating back to 1970,
are hidden in the grid, except for one... **can you work out who?**

```
M C L E I S H A B Y S Q D P C
A K A T L Y S H G E A T N O O
C R L K C A L B L S B P O I L
K L L E D O B R C M B P B U D
A B H U G H T O N A E E M R W
Y J D V S D C A V R L N Z T E
F R A N C I S D N K L D W I L
B J C M A E U H M D K R W R L
K F B I E O N U L F L E D A K
R S A X M I B R U C E Y G C J
A O R U W E H S P M O R G A N
L G R D A F M T I Y N G N M L
C B O N Q I C L T F A S H R E
H O N G T I L M J O R D T S X
G M I H Z S R S R E D N U A S
```

Lee **Clark**	Mick **Mills**	Lou **Macari**	Ron **Saunders**
Chris **Hughton**	Trevor **Francis**	Bill **Coldwell**	Norman **Bodell**
Alex **McLeish**	Barry **Fry**	Dave **Mackay**	Jim **Smith**
Eric **Black**	Trevor **Morgan**	Garry **Pendrey**	Sir Alf **Ramsey**
Steve **Bruce**	Kevan **Broadhurst**	John **Bond**	Willie **Bell**
Jim **Barron**	Terry **Cooper**	Keith **Leonard**	Freddie **Goodwin**

ANSWERS ON PAGE 6

22 ANDY
SHINNIE

PLAYER
OF THE YEAR

Curtis Davies

Curtis Davies was a deserving winner of the club's 2012-13 Player of the Season award and also collected the Players' Player of the Year award. A commanding central defender who skippered the side in the absence of Stephen Carr and Steve Caldwell, Davies consistently displayed his top flight quality with a series of assured performances.

His contribution didn't go unnoticed as ex-Blues boss Steve Bruce - once a centre back himself - signed him for promoted Hull City in June 2013. Although the fee was undisclosed, Blues were reported to have received a fee in the region of £2.3m which of course is vital to the continued progress of the club.

Davies played 41 league games in 2012-13, 44 in all competitions. Indicative of the defender's experience and ability is the fact that in all of those games he picked up a mere four yellow cards.

Davies contributed an excellent half dozen goals with all six of them coming against just three clubs - all of whom begin with a letter B: Blackpool, Burnley and Barnsley. Blues never lost when Davies scored. His goals earned points in 1-1 draws with Burnley and home and away to Blackpool. He also found the back of the net in a 2-1 win at Burnley while a double from Davies brought Boxing Day joy in a 2-1 win at Barnsley.

Davies' 89 career appearances for Birmingham City is more than he has played for any other club in a career that has taken in: Luton Town, West Bromwich Albion, Aston Villa, and a loan spell with Leicester City.

Goalkeeper Jack Butland took Blues' Young Player of the Year award for 2012-13.

This drill is supposed to be fun!

You will be working on your heading and reaction skills without even realising it!

Make sure to take turns being the player in the middle!

YOU

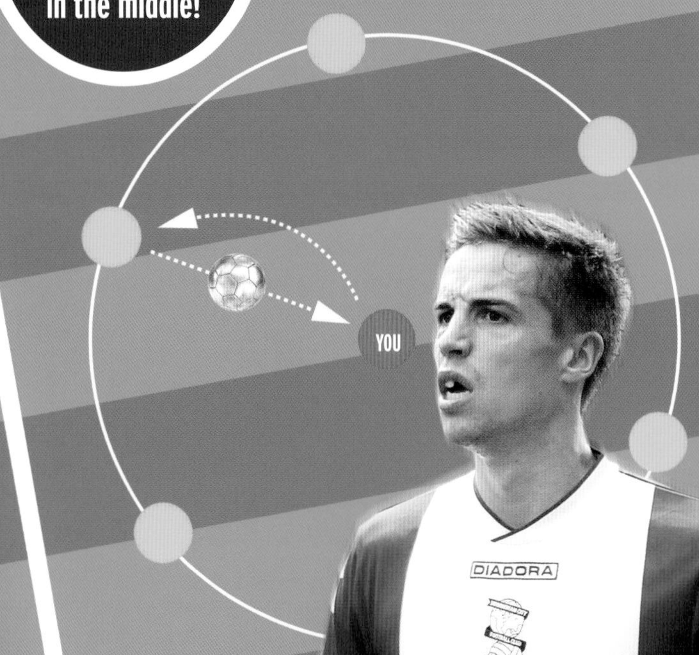

ave your mates
rm a circle around
ou, everyone facing you.
ou have the ball.

ASY

hrow the ball towards the other
layers' heads in turn, as if they
re going to head the ball.

'hile the ball is in the air, shout
IEAD' or 'CATCH' to whoever you
re directing the ball to. The player
ust then quickly react to your
ommand and perform the task
ou have shouted.

you yelled 'HEAD' the player
ust head the ball back to you.
you yelled 'CATCH' the player
ust catch the ball and return it.

a player performs the wrong
ask, that player sits and only
tanding players are still in the
ame. The last player standing
ins the round.

ARD

make this drill more difficult,
ave the players do the opposite
ask to what you have shouted,
.g. if you shout 'CATCH' they
ust 'HEAD' the ball.

lso start throwing the ball
players randomly, keeping
everyone on their toes
as they don't know whose
turn will be next!

HARDER

To develop this drill further, you can introduce other tasks - volley, chest trap or catch with your knees.

Can you think of any more to add?

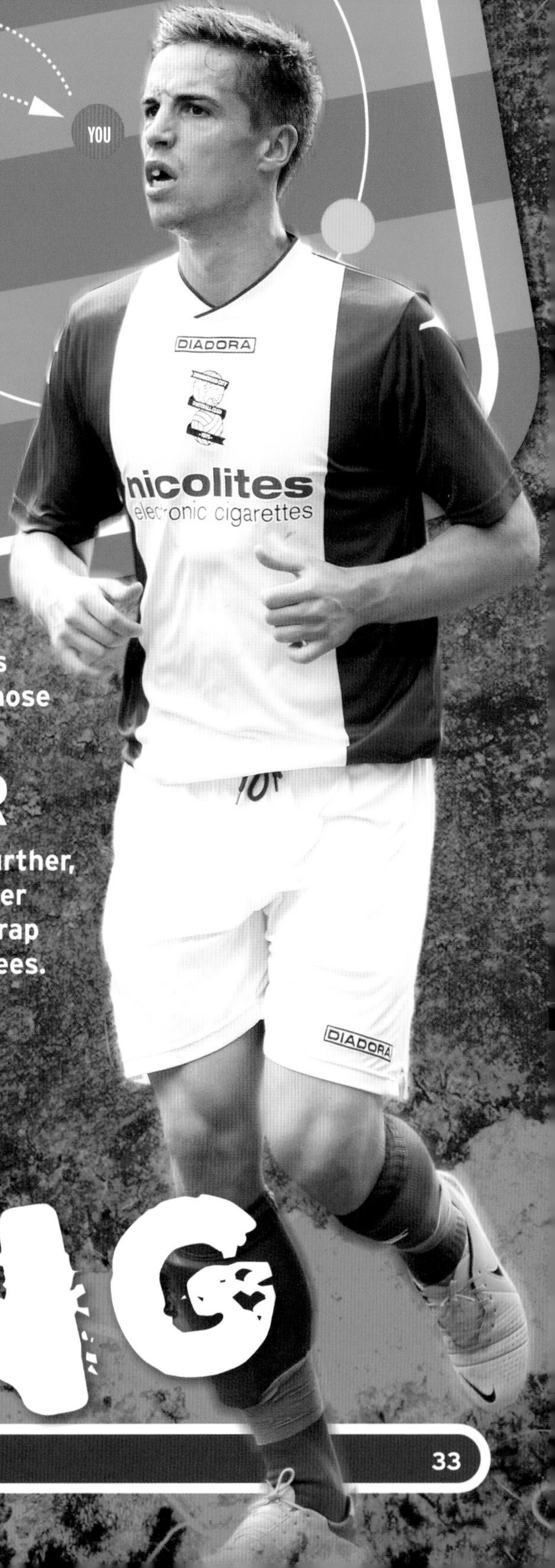

DIADORA
nicolites
electronic cigarettes
DIADORA

DRILLS: HEADING

ALEX McLEISH

November 2007 - June 2011

Put aside that McLeish left after the club showed faith in him and went to Villa. The bare fact is that in McLeish's spell in charge Blues beat Arsenal at Wembley to win the League Cup and achieved their highest league finish in half a century!

Relegated having arrived mid-way through 2007-08, McLeish won promotion in his first full season and the following December became the first Birmingham manager to ever win the top flight Manager of the Month award en route to a ninth place finish. February 2011 brought silverware and though relegation couldn't be averted McLeish left the club with the trophy cupboard in use.

TREVOR FRANCIS

May 1996 - December 2001

Like Gil Merrick, Trevor Francis had been a fabulous player for the club but also like Merrick his achievements as manager stand tall on their own merits. Playing attacking football befitting his own striker's instincts Francis missed out on a major trophy only by losing a penalty shoot out to Liverpool in the League Cup final of 2001.

Francis' team also deserved more from a trio of league campaigns which all ended in Play-off disappointment.

GAFFERS WALL OF FAME

ARTHUR TURNER · Nov 1954 - Feb 1958

Beating Liverpool 9-1 within a month of taking charge – having scored seven in the previous home game – augured well and Turner's side duly won Division Two (Now the Championship), reached the FA Cup Final the following year and the semi-final 12 months on (although never playing at home) while maintaining a healthy mid-table top flight position.

In his first full season, Turner became the first English manager to lead a team in a major European competition as Blues played in the Inter-Cities Fairs Cup. In that first campaign they lost to Barcelona in a semi-final replay after beating Inter Milan. Glorious days.

ARTHUR TURNER

GIL MERRICK

GIL MERRICK
May 1960 - April 1964

Not only was Gil Merrick the club's greatest ever player he enjoyed some incredible times as manager. Under Merrick Blues won the League Cup by beating Aston Villa in the 1963 final while he also led the club to the final of the Inter-Cities Fairs Cup, finishing runners' up to Roma in 1961. They had knocked out another Italian side in the semi's by beating Inter at the San Siro – a feat no other English team would match until 2008!

Merrick became manager straight after his 22 years as goalkeeper for the club. League success eluded the team under Merrick as they hovered just above the drop zone but a European final and a first trophy in 82 years mean that Merrick should be remembered as a manager as well as a player.

ALF JONES
July 1892 - June 1908

Alf Jones was Birmingham's first 'Secretary-manager' before his appointment the team was run by a committee. He'd already been secretary for seven years prior to his 16 year stint as secretary-manager. A local man, Jones was Blues through and through and was still watching virtually every home game until his death in 1930 when he was almost 80.

Nicknamed 'Inky' because he was always writing, Alf did much to establish Birmingham. It was during his spell in charge that the club joined the Football League and he also steered the club to an English (F.A.) Cup semi-final as well as a trio of promotions.

Can you spot the eight differences between the two action shots?

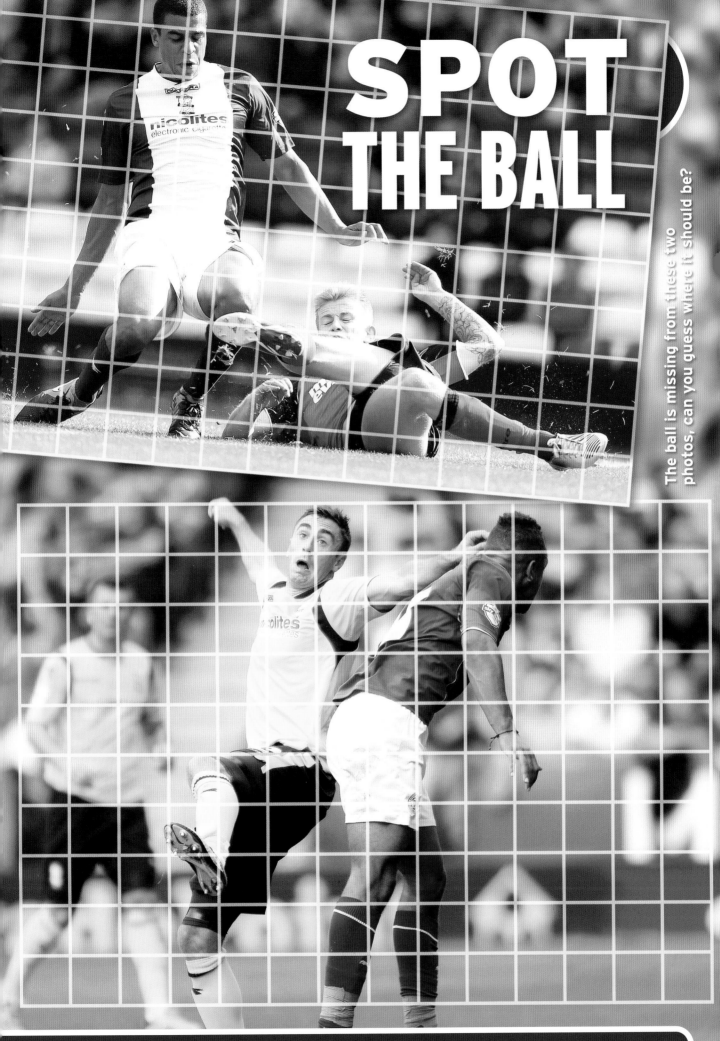

SPOT THE BALL

The ball is missing from these two photos, can you guess where it should be?

26 SCOTT
ALLAN

Can you... ...finish this picture of midfield maestro, **Scott Allan?**

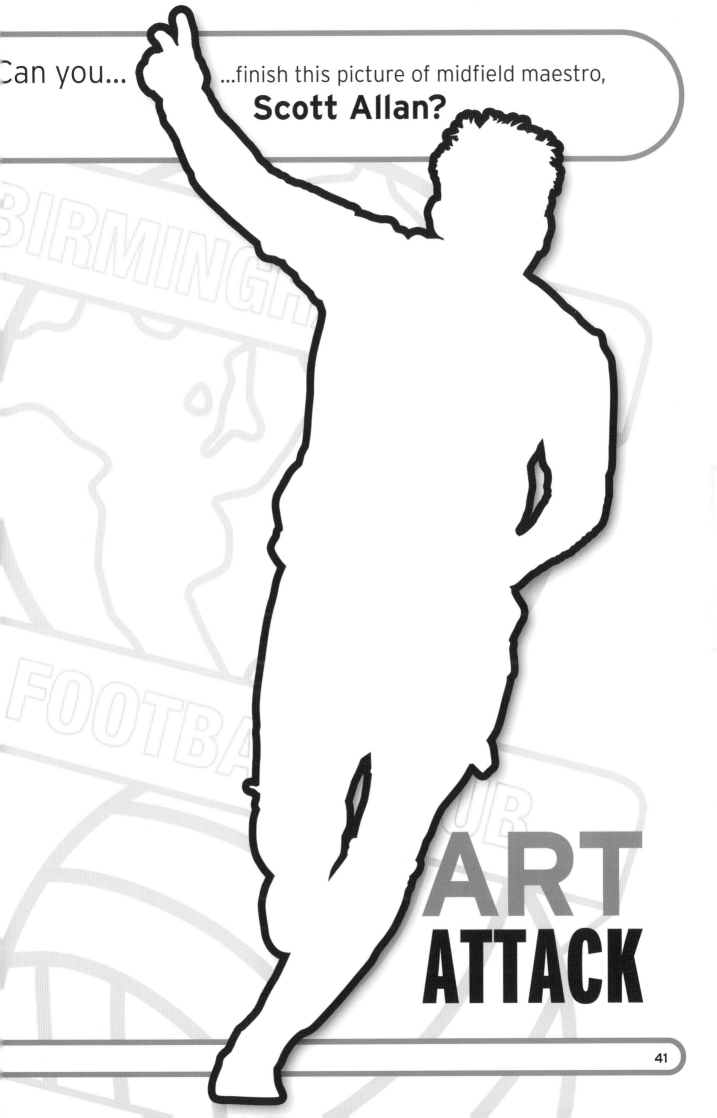

ART
ATTACK

Can you work out who these Blues players are?

ANSWERS ON PAGE 6.

GUESS WHO?

⑤

⑥

⑦

⑧

PAUL ROBINSON

YOUR TEAM MATES

Who is the best trainer? Me, obviously

Who has the worst dress sense?
Shane Ferguson and Scotty Allan

Who is the best dancer? Kyle Bartley

Who is the joker in the dressing room? Wade Elliott

Who spends longest in front of the mirror? Wade Elliott

FAVOURITES

Favourite actor?
Jason Statham

Favourite actress?
Sandra Bullock

Favourite movie? Gladiator

Favourite musician or band?
Justin Timberlake

Favourite place? Portugal

What are your pet hates? **I've got a few - losing, mess, I'm a bit OCD so like things to be tidy**

If you were a character in any movie, who would it be? **I'll have to be Jason Statham in Transporter**

What do you do on your days off? **Relax and chill out with the kids**

Snow or (Sun?)
(Coffee) or tea?
(Early bird) or night owl?
(Action) or comedy?
Apple or (Blackberry?)
(Cowboys) or aliens?
Sausage or (bacon?)
Cats or (dogs?)
Bond or (Bourne?)

What do you do on your days off? **Practice**

If not a footballer, what would you be? **Businessman a.k.a. Alan Sugar**

If you were a character in any movie, who would it be? **A minion out of 'Despicable Me'**

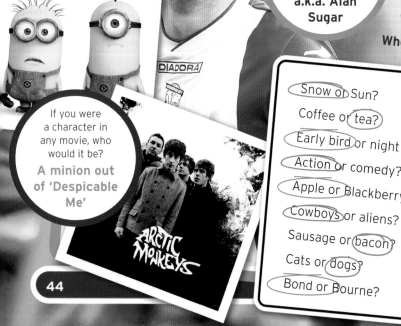

CALLUM REILLY

YOUR TEAM MATES

Who is the best trainer? Paul Robinson

Who has the worst dress sense? Shane Ferguson

Who is the best dancer? Will Packwood

Who is the joker in the dressing room? Paul Robinson

Who spends longest in front of the mirror? Wade Elliott

FAVOURITES

Favourite actor? Denzel Washington

Favourite actress? Mila Kunis

Favourite movie? The Business

Favourite musician or band? Arctic Monkeys

Favourite place? Dubai

(Snow) or Sun?
Coffee o (tea?)
(Early bird) or night owl?
(Action) or comedy?
Apple or (Blackberry?)
(Cowboys) or aliens?
Sausage or (bacon?)
Cats or (dogs?)
(Bond) or Bourne?

WILL PACKWOOD

YOUR TEAM MATES

Who is the best trainer? Paul Robinson

Who has the worst dress sense? Mitch Hancox

Who is the best dancer? Callum Reilly

Who is the joker in the dressing room? Paul Robinson

Who spends longest in front of the mirror? Pete Lovenkrands

FAVOURITES

Favourite actor? Tom Cruise

Favourite actress? Jessica Alba

Favourite movie? Dark Knight Rises

Favourite musician or band? Red Hot Chili Peppers

Favourite place? Boston

If you could trade places with someone for a day, who would it be?
Roger Federer

If not a footballer, what would you be?
Student

What are your pet hates?
There's nothing that really bugs me

Snow or (Sun?)
Coffee or (tea?)
(Early bird) or night owl?
Action or (comedy?)
(Apple) or Blackberry?
(Cowboys) or aliens?
Sausage or (bacon?)
Cats or (dogs?)
Bond or Bourne?

SCOTT ALLAN

YOUR TEAM MATES

Who is the best trainer? Paul Robinson

Who has the worst dress sense? Mitch Hancox

Who is the best dancer? Koby Arthur

Who is the joker in the dressing room? Me

Who spends longest in front of the mirror? Andy Shinnie

FAVOURITES

Favourite actor? Denzel Washington

Favourite actress? Halle Berry

Favourite movie? Man on Fire

Favourite musician or band? Oasis

Favourite place? Ibiza

If not a footballer, what would you be?
DJ

What are your pet hates?
People being late

If you could trade places with someone for a day, who would it be?
Ryan Gosling

Snow or (Sun?)
Coffee or (tea?)
(Early bird) or night owl?
Action or comedy?
(Apple) or Blackberry?
Cowboys or (aliens?)
Sausage or (bacon?)
Cats or (dogs?)
Bond or (Bourne?)

Who had squad number 4 before Paul Robinson?

11.

Who scored the last goal of the 2012-13 season?

12.

Who scored the first goal for Blues in the 2013-14 season?

13.

Neal Eardley completed his move to Blues on 1 July 2013, but which team did he come from?

14.

Which Blues defender celebrated their 27th birthday in March 2013?

15.

ANSWERS ON PAGE 62

Who scored the winner against Yeovil Town in August 2013?

16.

Who are Blues playing on New Year's Day 2014?

17.

Which four teams did Blues beat this summer in pre season friendlies?

18.

Who received the two red cards of last season?

19.

Blues signed attacking midfielder Andy Shinnie this summer. Which international team does he play for?

20.

BLUES 2-1 VILLA

LEAGUE CUP QUARTER FINAL, DECEMBER 1ST 2010

When Blues lifted the trophy after beating Arsenal at Wembley this victory that took Blues into the semi-final tasted even sweeter. With six minutes to play and the score level Cameron Jerome's ever willing running made something happen. Having gained possessio Jerome's cross found Nikola Zigic whose effort took a deflection and looped over stranded Villa 'keeper Brad Friedel to win the tie. In fact Blues had to protect their advantage for 12 minutes as six minutes injury time was negotiated.

Seb Larsson had put Blues ahead early on from the penalty spot after L Bowyer was tripped and Bowyer was involved in the equaliser too, being unable to prevent Gabriel Agbonlahor beating Ben Foster on the half hou That though was Villa's only bright spot on a night that saw Blues marc on to what would prove to be a successful end of the road.

JIMMY BLOOMFIELD

BLUES 3-1 VILLA

LEAGUE CUP FINAL 1ST LEG, MAY 23RD 1963

Four years before the League Cup Final was moved to Wembley, Aston Villa came to St. Andrew's for the first leg of the final and were despatched by a convincing victory. Four days later Blues capitalised on this win after a goalless second leg saw them receive the trophy at Villa Park. It was Birmingham's first ever major trophy and won on the home turf of the club's biggest local rivals, with captain Trevor Smith lifting the three-year-old trophy.

Ken Leek had scored twice when Villa were beaten 3-2 in the league at St. Andrew's earlier in the season and he'd also net twice on this greatest of occasions. Leek had already threatened before he opened the scoring in the 14th minute with a perfectly judged header from Bertie Auld's cross. The home side were well on top but went in level at the interval after Bobby Thomson scored for Villa in the 41st minute, giving 'keeper Johnny Schofield no chance.

Villa hadn't learned though and just seven minutes after the re-start the same combination of Auld and Leek opened them up for Leek's second. Jimmy Bloomfield had been injured in the first half but - this was before substitutes were allowed - continued with his leg strapped and got his reward when he scored what proved to be the last goal of the tie in the 66th minute.

BLUES 4-0 VILLA

DIVISION TWO, SEPTEMBER 21ST 1968

Blues had done the 'double' over Villa the previous season and this comprehensive victory really rubbed it in. Just four days earlier a home defeat had been suffered against a Bury side that would be relegated - if Stan Cullis' side had their eyes on the derby then it paid off, especially as the hammering of Villa was the first of fou wins in a row.

Blues bombarded Villa but had to wait until a 63rd minute goal from Phil Summerhill to open the scoring. Jimmy Greenhoff claimed the assist an three minutes later added his own name to the score-sheet with a neat header. Johnny Vincent made it 3-0 20 minutes later before Geoff Vowde wrapped up a great win after creating the second and third goals.

JIMMY GREENHOFF

or Blues fans it will always be the Second City derby against Aston Villa that is the most important but it's always nice to come out on top against West Bromwich Albion and Wolves too.

BARRY BRIDGES

BLUES 3-2 WOLVES

DIVISION TWO, DECEMBER 17TH 1966

This didn't look like it was going to be a great night. Wolves scored in the first minute through Dave Wagstaffe and doubled their lead 10 minutes before half time when Mike Bailey fired home from 30 yards. With 19 minutes to go most Blues fans would have been delighted with a draw but they were about to witness one of the all time great comebacks.

Goals from Barry Bridges and Mickey Bullock in the 71st and 79th minutes had Wolves rocking and having set up Bridges' goal to get Blues back into the match Geoff Vowden left the Wolves defence trailing in his wake as he burst clear to net a dramatic winner with two minutes to go and complete a first 'double' over Wolves in 46 years.

BLUES 4-0 BAGGIES

PREMIER LEAGUE, DECEMBER 18TH 2004

Steve Bruce's team liked to do their business early. A week earlier two goals in the first 12 minutes had set up a great away win over Villa and when West Bromwich Albion came to St. Andrew's, Blues opened the scoring in the fourth minute and were 3-0 to the good by the half hour mark.

Robbie Savage opened the scoring with a penalty after Bernt Haas fouled David Dunn and then two assists from Darren Carter created goals for Clinton Morrison and Emile Heskey.

Baggies' 'keeper Russell Hoult had a blinder in keeping the score respectable for Albion but he was powerless to stop Darren Anderton equalling their best ever league win over WBA with a late free kick.

DERBY HERO • KEN LEEK

To score a vital goal for Blues against Villa is the dream of many a fan. To score twice in the Second City derby in a cup final that brought Birmingham City their first ever major trophy makes Ken Leek a player every supporter should admire.

Signed from Newcastle United for £23,000 in 1961 Leek had played in the 1958 World Cup finals in Sweden for Wales. In a career that also saw him play for Northampton and Bradford City he totalled 147 goals in 397 games with a total of 61 in 120 games for Blues. He also played for Rhyl Town and Ton Petre.

Leek scored twice in the 1963 League Cup final first leg as Blues beat Villa 3-1 and went on to win the trophy. Ken's goals in the final took his tally to eight in the competition. Leek also scored 20 goals in the league that season - more than twice as many as anyone else - as relegation had only been avoided with victory in the last league fixture of the season, just four days before the first leg of the final.

Altogether Leek scored five goals in seven appearances for Blues against Villa.

The purpose of this drill is to focus on dribbling to beat a defender and finishing with a shot on goal.

Set up a square within shooting distance of your goal. Place a keeper in goal, and a defender inside the square. You and the rest of your mates are attackers and should start at the other side of the square from the goal.

Remember to take turns being in goal so that everyone gets a chance to play all positions!

EASY

Dribble into the square and try to beat the defender and dribble out of the opposite side of the square.

If you successfully dribble through the square without losing the ball to the defender, finish with a shot on goal!

If you lose the ball to the defender or dribble out either side of the square, you must then switch places with the defender so that you are protecting the square and they become an attacker.

The next player in line can go as soon as a shot on goal is taken or the defender has won the ball.

HARD

You can make the square bigger to make it easier for the attackers or make the square smaller to make it easier for the defenders.

HARDER

You can make the square slightly larger and add a second defender so that the game becomes 2 v 1 and harder for the attacker.

To make shooting harder, move the square further away from the goal and encourage a longer shot.

DRILLS: ATTACKING

4 PAUL
ROBINSON

MEET YOUR RIVALS

IPSWICH TOWN

GROUND: Portman Road CAPACITY: 30,311
MANAGER: Mick McCarthy NICKNAMES: The Blues, The Tractor Boys
DID YOU KNOW: Ipswich last appeared in the Premier League
in 2001-02, making them the Championships longest-serving club.

LEEDS UNITED

GROUND: Elland Road CAPACITY: 39,460
MANAGER: Brian McDermott NICKNAMES: The Whites, The Peacocks
DID YOU KNOW: Leeds United fans also have a salute
which is known as the 'Leeds Salute'.

LEICESTER CITY

GROUND: King Power Stadium CAPACITY: 32,262 MANAGER: Nigel Pearson
NICKNAMES: The Foxes, The Blues DID YOU KNOW: Leicester have been
FA Cup runners-up four times, which is a tournament record for the
most defeats in the final without having won the competition!

MIDDLESBROUGH

GROUND: Riverside Stadium CAPACITY: 34,988
MANAGER: Tony Mowbray NICKNAMES: Boro, the Smoggies
DID YOU KNOW: Middlesbrough won the League Cup in 2004,
the club's first and only major trophy.

MILLWALL

GROUND: The Den CAPACITY: 20,146 MANAGER: Steve Lomas
NICKNAME: The Lions DID YOU KNOW: Millwall are ranked as the fortieth
most successful club in English football - based on all results during the
club's 86 seasons in the Football League from 1920-21 to 2012-13.

NOTTINGHAM FOREST

GROUND: The City Ground CAPACITY: 30,602
MANAGER: Billy Davies NICKNAMES: Forest, The Reds
DID YOU KNOW: Nottingham Forest's most successful period came
under the management of Brian Clough, between 1975 and 1993.

QUEENS PARK RANGERS

GROUND: Loftus Road Stadium **CAPACITY:** 18,360
MANAGER: Harry Redknapp **NICKNAME:** The Hoops **DID YOU KNOW:** Rangers have had a somewhat nomadic existence, having played in 16 different locations throughout northwest London since their formation.

READING

GROUND: Madejski Stadium **CAPACITY:** 24,161
MANAGER: Nigel Adkins **NICKNAME:** The Royals
DID YOU KNOW: Established in 1871, Reading is one of the oldest teams in England.

SHEFFIELD WEDNESDAY

GROUND: Hillsborough Stadium **CAPACITY:** 39,732
MANAGER: Dave Jones **NICKNAMES:** The Owls, The Wednesday
DID YOU KNOW: Sheffield Wednesday were one of the founding members of The Premier League in 1992.

WATFORD

GROUND: Vicarage Road **CAPACITY:** 17,477
MANAGER: Gianfranco Zola **NICKNAME:** the Hornets
DID YOU KNOW: Sir Elton John serves alongside Graham Taylor as Watford's joint Honorary Life President.

WIGAN ATHLETIC

GROUND: DW Stadium **CAPACITY:** 25,138
MANAGER: Owen Coyle **NICKNAME:** Latics
DID YOU KNOW: Wigan will embark on its first European campaign during the 2013-14 season in the UEFA Europa League group stages.

YEOVIL TOWN

GROUND: Huish Park **CAPACITY:** 9,565 (5,212 seated)
MANAGER: Gary Johnson **NICKNAME:** The Glovers
DID YOU KNOW: Huish Park was built in 1990 and named after Yeovil's former home, Huish, whose pitch had an 2.4 metre sideline to sideline slope!

Do you think you're the expert in all things Birmingham City?
Take our Fact or Fib quiz and find out!

Beau Brummie was originally a French Bulldog.

1. FACT OR FIB?

St. Andrew's Stadium holds up to 28,000 fans.

2. FACT OR FIB?

Blues were founded in 1875 as Small Heath Alliance.

3. FACT OR FIB?

Nikola Zigic was born in Slovenia.

4. FACT OR FIB?

Before coming to Birmingham, Lee Clark was manger at Huddersfield Town.

5. FACT OR FIB?

In the last game of 2013, Blues face Blackburn.

6. FACT OR FIB?

Wade Elliott is one of the best defenders Blues has seen, he made 38 league appearances last season.

7. FACT OR FIB?

Darren Randolph is a Republic of Ireland international but is also eligible to play for the USA.

8. FACT OR FIB?

Blues' longest-serving manager by matches was the great Trevor Francis. He served 275 matches.

9. FACT OR FIB?

Scott Allan joined Blues in July 2013 on a season-long loan.

10. FACT OR FIB?

FACT OR FIB?

Blues' fiercest rivalry is with Aston Villa, with whom we play the Second City derby.

11. FACT OR FIB?

Blues' highest goalscorer last season was Nikola Zigic.

12. FACT OR FIB?

Birmingham City's president is Carson Yeung, he is from Hong Kong.

13. FACT OR FIB?

Striker, Lee Novak, celebrated his 26th birthday this September.

14. FACT OR FIB?

Birmingham City Ladies won the FA Women's Cup in 2012.

15. FACT OR FIB?

Koby Arthur is a midfielder from Kumasi, Ghana.

16. FACT OR FIB?

Gil Merrick was a great Blues manager of the 1970s.

17. FACT OR FIB?

Will Packwood is an American defender, born in California in 1993.

18. FACT OR FIB?

Birmingham City have won the League Cup twice, once in 2011 and once in 1963.

19. FACT OR FIB?

Joe Bradford is Blues' top goalscorer with 235 league goals.

20. FACT OR FIB?

ANSWERS ON PAGE 62

CLUB &

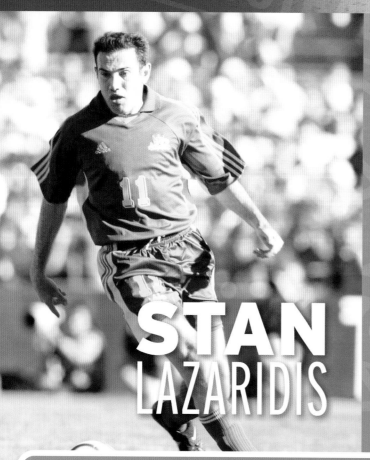

- **Won 25 caps for England while with Birmingham.**
- A goalkeeper, Harry Hibbs kept 10 clean sheets in those games.
- He played 389 times for Blues and had a testimonial against Villa.
- Played in the 1931 FA Cup final against WBA whose 'keeper was Harry's cousin Harold Pearson.

Hibbs won more caps for England while with Blues than any other player - two more even than fellow goalkeeper Gil Merrick.

Hibbs was the perfect kind of goalkeeper, unspectacular because his positional sense was so good. At the club between 1924 and 1940. Later manager of Walsall who he took to the Third Division (South) Final in 1946 at Stamford Bridge -the same ground where he'd made his England debut in 1929.

HARRY HIBBS

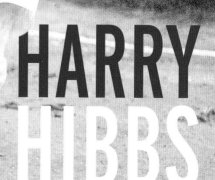

- Won 33 caps for Australia while with Blues, at the time becoming the club's most capped player.
- Named in Australia's squad for the 2006 World Cup although had to withdraw.
- Scored the winner in a 2003 derby day with Villa.
- Scored eight goals in 222 games in seven years.

An Aussie with an eye-catching change of pace. Lazaridis could operate effectively anywhere on the left flank and part of the 2002 promotion winning team, playing in the Play-off Final at the Millennium Stadium. He'd played at the same ground the previous season against Liverpool in the League Cup Final.

After returning 'Down Under', Lazaridis registered positive for a drugs test in January 2007. His previous good character was noted but he was banned for 12 months.

STAN LAZARIDIS

COUNTRY

Blues' all-time most capped player.

Won over 50 of his 88 Northern Ireland caps while with Blues but was actually born in Germany.

Originally signed for Birmingham on loan in 2003 before a £1.5m fee to Fulham secured him in January 2004.

Named as 'keeper in a fans' best Premier League team in 2003-04.

A great all-round goalkeeper who when he was at Fulham was described as 'the best taker of a cross in Britain' by his manager Kevin Keegan.

Born in Germany to German and English parents Maik qualified for Northern Ireland due to a rule that allows UK citizens born outside of the UK to represent any of the home nations.

MAIK TAYLOR

Won the first 12 of his 52 England caps with Birmingham City.

Part of England's squad at the 1982 World Cup.

Became England's first £1m player when sold to Nottingham Forest in 1979.

Scored 15 goals in his first 16 games for Blues including four goals in a game as a 16 year old!

A sensational player from the moment he burst onto the scene as a 16-year-old with electrifying pace, 133 of Trevor's career total of 225 goals were scored for Blues for whom he made 330 of his 752 career appearances.

His most famous goal was the winner in the 1979 European Cup final for Forest against Malmo but the one Blues fans recall above all others was against QPR when he beat four men and fired home from 25 yards.

In addition to his splendid career in England for club and country Francis also played in the USA, Italy, Scotland and Australia winning trophies in the first three. He returned to St. Andrew's as manager from 1996 to 2001.

TREVOR FRANCIS

7 CHRIS BURKE

Beau Brummie can't play football until he's done his homework, and he's stuck!

Can you help him?

Using the numbers of the BCFC squad can you work out the answers to the following sums?

For example, Hayden Mullins is No. 8 and Darren Ambrose is No. 10 so Hayden Mullins + Darren Ambrose is 18.

Dan Burn	**+**	**Wade Elliott**	**=**	
2 **Scott Allan**	**+**	**Koby Arthur**	**=**	
3 **Mitch Hancox**	**-**	**Chris Burke**	**=**	
4 **Andy Shinnie**	**-**	**Lee Novak**	**=**	
5 **Paul Robinson**	**X**	**David Murphy**	**=**	
6 **Kyle Bartley**	**X**	**Will Packwood**	**=**	
7 **Olly Lee**	**÷**	**Neal Eardley**	**=**	
8 **Nikola Zigic**	**÷**	**Darren Randolph**	**=**	

THE SQUAD

1	Darren Randolph	12	Lee Novak	22	Andrew Shinnie
2	Neal Eardley	13	Colin Doyle	23	Jonathan Spector
3	David Murphy	14	Will Packwood	24	Tom Adeyemi
4	Paul Robinson	15	Wade Elliott	25	Matt Green
5	Kyle Bartley	16	Koby Arthur	26	Scott Allan
6	Dan Burn	17	Callum Reilly	27	Shane Ferguson
7	Christopher Burke	18	Mitchell Hancox	28	Ryan Higgins
8	Hayden Mullins	19	Nikola Zigic	29	Reece Brown
0	Darren Ambrose	20	Olly Lee	30	Nick Townsend
1	Peter Lovenkrands	21	Akwasi Asante	31	Paul Caddis

ANSWERS ON PAGE 62

2014 PREDICTIONS

Premier League winner...
Chelsea

YOUR PREDICTION

Premier League runner-up...
Man United

YOUR PREDICTION

Premier League top scorer...
Dimitar Berbatov

YOUR PREDICTION

Championship winner...
QPR

YOUR PREDICTION

Championship runner-up...
Blackpool

YOUR PREDICTION

FA Cup winner...
Arsenal

YOUR PREDICTION

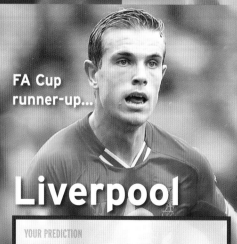

FA Cup runner-up...
Liverpool

YOUR PREDICTION

Championship top scorer...
Troy Deeney

YOUR PREDICTION

Here are our predictions for the new year...

Do you agree with us?!

First manager to get the sack in 2014...

Alan Pardew

YOUR PREDICTION

First player booked for taking their top off in 2014...

Luis Suarez

YOUR PREDICTION

First player to get sent off in 2014...

Joey Barton

YOUR PREDICTION

First Blues player to score three goals in 2014...

Andy Shinnie

YOUR PREDICTION

Blues player to make the most appearances this season...

Paul Robinson

YOUR PREDICTION

First player to score a hat-trick in 2014...

Miguel Michu

YOUR PREDICTION

League Cup Winner...

Everton

YOUR PREDICTION

2014 Manager of the Year...

Lee Clark

YOUR PREDICTION

ANSWERS

PAGE 21
WILD ABOUT FOOTIE

1. Derby County, 2. Hull, 3. Sunderland, 4. Sheffield Wednesday, 5. Norwich, 6. Watford, 7. Wolverhampton Wanderers, 8. Newcastle United, 9. Leicester City, 10. Millwall

PAGE 23
FACE OFF

1. Koby Arthur, 2. Scott Allan, 3. Dan Burn, 4. Tom Adeyemi, 5. Will Packwood, 6. Lee Novak, 7. Chris Burke, 8. Wade Elliott, 9. Jonathan Spector

PAGE 26
BIG FAT QUIZ OF THE YEAR 2013 · PART 1

1. Marlon King, 2. Marlon King, 3. Jack Butland, 4. Wade Elliott, 5. 19.630 vs Wolverhampton Wanderers, 1 April 2013, 6. Barnet, 7. 16, 8. Darren Ambrose, 9. Wade Elliott and Paul Robinson, 10. 12th

PAGE 30
CAN YOU MANAGE?

Barry Fry

PAGE 34
BLUES GOT TALENT

Olly Murs, Ed Sheeran, Robin Thicke, Emeli Sande and Rita Ora

PAGE 38
SPOT THE DIFFERENCE

PAGE 39
SPOT THE BALL

PAGE 42
GUESS WHO?

1. Tom Adeyemi, 2. Scott Allan, 3. Paul Robinson, 4. Lee Novak, 5. Neal Eardley, 6. Andy Shinnie, 7. Chris Burke, 8. Wade Elliott

PAGE 46
BIG FAT QUIZ OF THE YEAR 2013 · PART 2

11. Steven Caldwell, 12. Ravel Morrison, 13. Scott Allan, 14. Blackpool, 15. Jonathan Spector, 16. Daniel Seaborne (o.g.), 17. Barnsley, 18. Alfreton Town, Shamrock Rovers, Swindon Town and Hull City, 19. Nikola Zigic, 20. Scotland

PAGE 54
FACT OR FIB?

1. False, 2. False, 30,016, 3. True, 4. False, Serbia, 5. True, 6. True, 7. False, Elliott is a midfielder, 8. True, 9. False 290 matches, 10. True, 11. True, 12. False, Marlon King, 13. True, 14. False, it was his 25th birthday, 15. True, 16. True, 17. False, 1960s, 18. False, he was born in Massachusetts, 19. True, 20. False, 249

PAGE 59
BEAU BRUMMIE'S SUMS

1. $6 + 15 = 21$, 2. $26 + 16 = 42$, 3. $18 - 7 = 11$, 4. $22 - 12 = 10$, 5. $4 \times 3 = 12$, 6. $5 \times 14 = 70$, 7. $20 \div 2 = 10$, 8. $19 \div 1 = 19$